A GUIDE
TO RELOCATING TO GREECE
EMBRACE THE MEDITERRANEAN DREAM
BY
WILLIAM JONES
2023

A Guide to Relocating to Greece: Embrace the Mediterranean Dream
By William Jones
This edition was created and published by Mamba Press
©MambaPress 2023

Contents

Preface
- Introduction
- Chapter 1: The Greek Dream - Why Move to Greece?
- Chapter 2: Preparing for Your Greek Adventure
- Chapter 3: Choosing Your Greek Destination
- Chapter 4: Finding Your Greek Home
- Chapter 5: Navigating Greek Bureaucracy
- Chapter 6: Employment and Entrepreneurship in Greece
- Chapter 7: Education and Schools
- Chapter 8: Embracing Greek Culture
- Chapter 9: Exploring Greek Cuisine
- Chapter 10: Staying Safe and Healthy
- Chapter 11: Navigating Daily Life
- Chapter 12: Enjoying Your Greek Adventure
- Conclusion
- Appendix: Resources and Useful Information

Preface

Greece, the land of myths, legends, and epic histories, has beckoned travelers and adventurers for centuries. From the shimmering waters of the Aegean to the majestic peaks of Mount Olympus, Greece boasts a natural beauty that is nothing short of breathtaking. Its rich tapestry of culture and history has woven a narrative that spans millennia, leaving an indelible mark on the world.

But Greece is more than just a destination for tourists; it's a place where dreams come alive, where reality blends seamlessly with fantasy. It's a place where one can immerse themselves in the embrace of the Mediterranean lifestyle, savoring slow meals under the shade of ancient olive trees, and feeling the sand between their toes on sun-drenched beaches.

The decision to move to Greece is not just about changing your address; it's about embracing a new way of life, a different perspective, and a chance to craft your own narrative against the backdrop of this timeless land. It's about learning to dance the sirtaki, mastering the art of souvlaki, and finding tranquility in the shade of whitewashed buildings with cobalt-blue accents.

As you hold this guide in your hands, you are embarking on a journey that could redefine the course of your life. Whether you're drawn to Greece by the promise of adventure, the allure of its history, the warmth of its people, or simply the magnetic pull of the Mediterranean, this book is your trusted companion on this odyssey.

Moving to Greece is a thrilling prospect, but it's not without its challenges and complexities. This guide aims to demystify the process, providing you with a roadmap to navigate the bureaucratic hurdles, cultural nuances, and practical considerations that come with relocating to this enchanting country.

In the chapters that follow, you'll find a wealth of information to help you prepare for your Greek adventure. We'll explore the legal requirements for residency and visas, delve into the intricacies of the Greek healthcare system, and offer insights into finding the perfect place to call home. We'll also discuss employment opportunities, education options, and ways to immerse yourself in Greek culture.

While this guide offers practical advice, it's essential to remember that Greece is a place where experiences often defy expectations. It's a country where spontaneity is celebrated, and where moments of serendipity can lead to the most memorable adventures. It's a place where the concept of "philoxenia" (hospitality) runs deep, and where you'll find that strangers quickly become friends.

As you read through these pages, keep in mind that your journey to Greece is unique. While this guide can provide valuable insights and guidance, it's your spirit of exploration and your willingness to embrace the unknown that will make your experience truly remarkable.

So, whether you're planning a permanent move, a seasonal escape, or even just considering the possibility of a new chapter in Greece, let this book be your compass. Let it inspire you to take that leap of faith, to chase your Mediterranean dreams, and to find your own piece of paradise in this extraordinary country.

May the Greek winds carry you to uncharted shores, and may the spirit of Greece fill your heart with joy, curiosity, and wonder.

Kalí týchi! (Good luck!)

Introduction

Greece, a land of ancient wonders and modern marvels, beckons to those who seek adventure, culture, and the undeniable allure of the Mediterranean lifestyle. This introduction sets the stage for the journey that lies ahead—a journey into the heart of Greece, a country where myth and reality intertwine, where history lives and breathes, and where the warmth of its people is as legendary as its ancient ruins.

The Allure of Greece

Picture it: You're standing on the rocky shores of Santorini, gazing out at the endless expanse of the azure Aegean Sea. The sun dips below the horizon, casting a golden hue over the iconic whitewashed buildings that cling to the cliffs. The scent of grilled seafood wafts from a nearby taverna, and the sound of laughter and music fills the air. This is Greece—an intoxicating blend of natural beauty, culture, and hospitality that has captured the hearts of travelers for centuries.

Greece is a land where the past and present coexist harmoniously. It's a place where ancient temples and archaeological wonders stand as testament to the grandeur of empires long gone, while bustling cities and modern infrastructure thrive with the energy of a dynamic nation. From the majestic Acropolis in Athens to the mystical ruins of Delphi and the awe-inspiring monasteries of Meteora, Greece's historical legacy is a living, breathing part of its landscape.

Yet, Greece is not just a museum of antiquity; it's a vibrant and evolving country with a rich tapestry of traditions, festivals, and cultural celebrations. The Greek people are known for their zest for life, their love of food, and their unbreakable spirit, even in the face of adversity. To move to Greece is to immerse yourself in this cultural tapestry, to become a part of a society that values community, family, and the simple joys of life.

The Mediterranean Dream

Moving to Greece isn't merely a change of location; it's an embrace of a different way of life—a Mediterranean dream that has lured countless individuals and families from around the world. It's a dream of basking in the Mediterranean sun, enjoying long, leisurely meals with friends and family, and living at a pace that allows you to savor every moment.

The Mediterranean way of life is characterized by a sense of "joie de vivre," a profound appreciation for the present moment. It's about taking time to enjoy a cup of Greek coffee at a café, strolling through ancient olive groves, and sipping on ouzo as the sun sets over the sea. It's a lifestyle that values the connections between people, the importance of food, and the beauty of the natural world.

For many, the decision to move to Greece is a chance to step off the treadmill of modern life, to escape the rush and embrace a more relaxed and fulfilling existence. It's an opportunity to recalibrate your priorities, to reconnect with nature, and to discover what truly matters to you.

Benefits and Challenges of Living in Greece

Like any major life decision, moving to Greece comes with its own set of benefits and challenges. It's essential to approach this adventure with your eyes wide open, understanding both the rewards and the complexities that await.

Benefits of Living in Greece

1. **Natural Beauty**: Greece boasts some of the most stunning landscapes in the world, from pristine beaches to rugged mountains and idyllic islands. The country's diverse geography means there's always a new corner to explore.
2. **Cultural Richness**: Greece's history is a tapestry of civilizations, from the Minoans to the Romans, Byzantines, and Ottomans. This heritage is celebrated in every aspect of Greek life, from architecture to art and cuisine.
3. **Health Benefits**: The Mediterranean diet, with its emphasis on fresh vegetables, olive oil, and lean proteins, is renowned for its

health benefits. Greece's clean air and outdoor lifestyle also contribute to overall well-being.
4. **Community and Hospitality**: Greeks are known for their warmth and hospitality. Building relationships and forming a sense of community is an integral part of life in Greece.
5. **Cultural Experiences**: Greece's festivals, celebrations, and traditions provide a constant source of cultural enrichment. From Orthodox Easter to village panigíria (festivals), there's always something to celebrate.

Challenges of Living in Greece

1. **Bureaucracy**: Greece has a reputation for bureaucracy and administrative challenges. Navigating the paperwork required for residency, healthcare, and other matters can be frustrating.
2. **Economic Uncertainty**: Greece has faced economic challenges in recent years, which have affected employment opportunities and the cost of living in some areas.
3. **Language Barrier**: While many Greeks speak English, particularly in tourist areas, a basic knowledge of Greek is essential for day-to-day life and forming deeper connections with locals.
4. **Seasonal Tourism**: Greece's economy relies heavily on tourism, which means that some areas may become crowded during the tourist season and quieter during the off-season.
5. **Adjustment Period**: Moving to a new country always involves an adjustment period. You may experience culture shock and homesickness, but these are natural phases of the expat experience.

Identifying Your Motivations and Goals

Before embarking on your journey to Greece, it's crucial to clarify your motivations and goals. What is it that draws you to this Mediterranean paradise? Are you seeking a change of scenery, a slower pace of life, or a deeper connection with Greek culture and heritage? Understanding your reasons for making this move will help you make informed decisions along the way.

Perhaps you're dreaming of waking up to the sound of the waves lapping at the shore, or maybe you're envisioning afternoons spent sipping Greek wine at a seaside taverna. Your motivations could be driven by a desire to explore the history and archaeology of Greece or to embark on a new career or business venture in this vibrant country.

By the end of this journey, you'll not only have a clearer understanding of Greece as a place to live but also a deeper understanding of yourself and what you hope to achieve through this transformative experience.

Navigating the Greek Odyssey

As you read through the following chapters, you'll embark on a comprehensive exploration of what it takes to move to Greece. We'll delve into the practical aspects, such as legal requirements, financial planning, and healthcare considerations. We'll guide you through the process of finding the perfect place to live and offer insights into employment and entrepreneurship in Greece. You'll also discover how to navigate the Greek education system, embrace the local culture, and make the most of your daily life in Greece.

But remember, while this guide provides valuable information, your journey will be uniquely your own. Greece has a way of capturing hearts and forging unforgettable memories. Embrace the Mediterranean way of life, savor each moment, and let the beauty and culture of Greece enrich your life in ways you never imagined.

May this book be your trusted companion, offering guidance and inspiration as you make your dreams of living in Greece a reality. Whether you're drawn to the bustling streets of Athens, the tranquil shores of Crete, or the charming villages of the Peloponnese, Greece welcomes you with open arms.

Kalí týchi! (Good luck!)

The Greek Dream - Why Move to Greece?

Greece, the land of gods and philosophers, poets and warriors, has a magnetic allure that has beckoned people from across the globe for centuries. But what is it about this ancient and sun-drenched country that inspires such fascination, and why do so many dream of making Greece their home?

A Land of Timeless Beauty

One of the most compelling reasons to move to Greece is its breathtaking natural beauty. From the rugged mountains of the mainland to the idyllic islands dotting the Aegean and Ionian Seas, Greece offers a diverse and captivating landscape.

Imagine yourself hiking through the Samaria Gorge in Crete, where sheer cliffs rise on either side, or standing atop the rocky spires of Meteora, where monasteries seem to defy gravity. Picture a leisurely sail through the Cyclades, with their pristine beaches and whitewashed buildings. Greece's geography is a playground for outdoor enthusiasts, with opportunities for hiking, biking, sailing, and more.

The Mediterranean climate is another draw. Greece enjoys long, warm summers and mild winters, making it an ideal destination for those seeking sun and pleasant weather year-round. The sun-drenched landscapes and crystal-clear waters of the Greek islands are the stuff of postcards and daydreams.

A Cradle of Civilization

Greece's historical significance is impossible to overstate. It is, after all, the birthplace of Western civilization. From the ancient Minoans on Crete to the classical era of Athens and the grandeur of the Hellenistic period, Greece's history is a tapestry woven with threads of philosophy, art, literature, and science.

Visiting Greece is like stepping back in time. The Acropolis of Athens, crowned by the Parthenon, is a symbol of human achievement and a testament to the enduring power of ancient ideas. Delve deeper, and you'll discover the ruins of ancient theaters, the oracle of Delphi, and the palace of Knossos, each offering a glimpse into the past.

Living in Greece means having the opportunity to immerse yourself in this rich history. It means walking in the footsteps of philosophers like Socrates and Aristotle, exploring archaeological sites, and engaging with a culture that reveres its heritage.

A Culinary Odyssey

Greek cuisine is celebrated worldwide for its freshness, flavor, and healthfulness. It's no wonder that food is a central part of the Greek way of life. From the simplicity of a Greek salad, with its ripe tomatoes, creamy feta, and tangy olives, to the succulence of grilled souvlaki and the indulgence of baklava, Greek food is a revelation for the senses.

Imagine dining alfresco at a seaside taverna, savoring the catch of the day, grilled octopus, and a carafe of local wine as the sun sets over the water. Or picture yourself in a traditional Greek village, where you can sample homemade dishes passed down through generations.

The Mediterranean diet, characterized by fresh vegetables, olive oil, and lean proteins, is not just delicious—it's also recognized for its health benefits. Greece's abundance of fresh produce, seafood, and olive groves means that you'll have access to some of the world's best ingredients for a healthy and enjoyable life.

Warmth and Philoxenia

Greeks are renowned for their hospitality, which they call "philoxenia." It's a concept deeply ingrained in the culture—a commitment to welcoming guests with open arms and making them feel at home. Whether you're a tourist or a new resident, you'll experience this warmth firsthand.

Imagine arriving in a Greek village and being greeted by your neighbors with gifts of fresh produce, invitations to their homes, and offers of help to settle in. The sense of community in Greece is strong, and it's not uncommon to form deep bonds with your neighbors and fellow villagers.

The spirit of philoxenia extends to everyday interactions as well. You'll find that strangers quickly become friends, and a simple greeting can lead to a warm conversation. Greeks value relationships and connections, and forming meaningful friendships is an integral part of life in Greece.

A Relaxed Pace of Life

Life in Greece is not rushed; it's savored. The concept of "kefi," which roughly translates to "spirit" or "joy of life," permeates the culture. It's about taking the time to enjoy a cup of Greek coffee at a café, lingering over a meal with friends, and relishing the small pleasures of life.

The Mediterranean lifestyle encourages a slower pace—a focus on quality over quantity. It's about spending time with loved ones, connecting with nature, and finding contentment in the present moment. While this way of life may take some adjustment for those accustomed to the hustle and bustle of urban centers, it offers a profound sense of well-being and fulfillment.

Imagine waking up in the morning to the gentle sound of waves lapping at the shore, sipping a frappe at a seaside café, and strolling through ancient olive groves in the afternoon. In Greece, you'll find that each day is an opportunity to enjoy the simple pleasures that make life meaningful.

A Sense of Adventure

Moving to Greece is not without its challenges, but it's also an adventure waiting to unfold. It's an opportunity to step out of your comfort zone, embrace the unknown, and discover new facets of yourself.

Imagine navigating the bustling streets of Athens, where ancient and modern collide, or embarking on a road trip through the Greek countryside, where hidden villages and pristine landscapes await. Picture yourself learning the Greek language, mastering the art of making moussaka, and participating in local festivals that celebrate life's abundance.

The Greek dream is not just about a change of scenery; it's about a change of perspective. It's about embracing a new way of life, a different rhythm, and a deeper connection with the world around you. It's about forging your own path, writing your own story, and finding your place in the rich tapestry of Greece.

Closing Thoughts

The dream of moving to Greece is as diverse as the people who pursue it. Some are drawn by the promise of a sun-soaked retirement, while others seek adventure, cultural enrichment, or the opportunity to start a new chapter in their lives. Whatever your motivation, Greece offers a wealth of experiences and opportunities waiting to be explored.

In the chapters that follow, we'll dive deeper into the practical aspects of moving to Greece—legal requirements, financial planning, healthcare considerations, and more. We'll guide you through the process of finding the perfect place to live, whether it's on a bustling island or in a tranquil village. You'll also discover insights into employment and entrepreneurship, education options, and how to immerse yourself in Greek culture.

As you read on, keep in mind that Greece is a place where experiences often defy expectations. It's a country where spontaneity is celebrated, where moments of serendipity can lead to the most memorable adventures. It's a place where the concept of "philoxenia" (hospitality) runs deep, and where you'll find that strangers quickly become friends.

The journey to Greece is not just a change of location; it's a transformation of the soul. It's an opportunity to embrace the Mediterranean dream, to savor each moment, and to let the beauty and culture of Greece enrich your life in ways you never imagined.

So, whether you're planning a permanent move, a seasonal escape, or even just considering the possibility of a new chapter in Greece, let this chapter be your inspiration. Let it remind you of the countless reasons why Greece has captured the hearts of so many, and let it ignite your own Greek dream.

Kalí týchi! (Good luck!)

Preparing for Your Greek Adventure

The decision to move to Greece is an exciting and life-altering one. It holds the promise of a new beginning in a country known for its natural beauty, rich history, and warm hospitality. However, like any significant life change, moving to Greece requires careful preparation and planning to ensure a smooth transition. In this chapter, we'll delve into the essential steps you need to take to prepare for your Greek adventure.

Legal Requirements and Visas

Before you can embark on your journey to Greece, you must first navigate the legal requirements and obtain the necessary visas and permits. The specific visa you need will depend on your nationality, the purpose of your move, and the duration of your stay. Here are some common visa options:

1. **Tourist Visa**: If you're planning a short stay for tourism or exploration, you may not need a visa, depending on your nationality. Typically, tourists from EU member countries and many other nations are granted entry for up to 90 days within a 180-day period without a visa.
2. **Residence Permit**: For those seeking to live in Greece long-term, you'll need a residence permit. This permit can be obtained for various reasons, such as employment, family reunification, or retirement.
3. **Work Visa**: If you plan to work in Greece, you'll need a work visa. It's essential to secure a job offer before applying for this type of visa, as your employer will play a significant role in the application process.
4. **Student Visa**: If you intend to study in Greece, you'll require a student visa. You'll need to provide proof of acceptance at a Greek educational institution, along with other necessary documents.

5. **Retirement Visa**: Greece offers a special visa for retirees. To qualify, you typically need to meet certain age and income requirements.

The visa application process can be complex and time-consuming, so it's advisable to start well in advance of your planned move. Be sure to gather all the required documents, such as proof of income, health insurance, and a clean criminal record, and submit your application to the Greek consulate or embassy in your home country.

Financial Planning and Budgeting

Moving to Greece also involves financial planning to ensure you can support yourself and your family comfortably. Here are some financial considerations to keep in mind:

1. **Cost of Living**: Research the cost of living in your chosen destination in Greece. Major cities like Athens and Thessaloniki may have higher living costs than smaller towns and villages.
2. **Currency Exchange**: Familiarize yourself with the currency exchange rates and banking systems in Greece. You may need to open a local bank account once you arrive.
3. **Income and Employment**: If you're planning to work in Greece, ensure you have a job or a source of income lined up before your move. It's essential to understand your employment contract and salary details.
4. **Healthcare Costs**: Greece has a public healthcare system, but many residents also opt for private health insurance. Research the healthcare options available to you and budget for insurance premiums and potential medical expenses.
5. **Property Costs**: If you plan to purchase property in Greece, consider the costs associated with real estate transactions, such as property taxes and legal fees.
6. **Taxes**: Understand Greece's tax system and how it may impact

your financial situation, including any tax obligations in your home country.

Creating a comprehensive budget that takes into account all your expected expenses will help you better plan for your new life in Greece. It's also wise to have some financial reserves for unexpected costs or emergencies.

Healthcare and Insurance Considerations

Access to quality healthcare is a crucial aspect of your relocation. Greece offers a public healthcare system known as the National Healthcare System (EOPYY), which provides essential medical services. However, many residents also opt for private health insurance to access a broader range of healthcare facilities and services.

Here are some important healthcare and insurance considerations:

1. **European Health Insurance Card (EHIC)**: If you're an EU citizen, you should obtain the EHIC, which provides access to emergency and necessary healthcare services in Greece. However, it's not a substitute for comprehensive health insurance.
2. **Private Health Insurance**: Many expats in Greece choose to supplement the public healthcare system with private health insurance. This can provide you with quicker access to specialists and private clinics.
3. **Pharmacies**: Greece has an extensive network of pharmacies, and many common medications are available over the counter. Prescription medications are also accessible with a doctor's prescription.
4. **Emergency Services**: Greece has a well-developed emergency healthcare system, with ambulance services and hospitals equipped to handle a range of medical emergencies.

Before your move, it's essential to research health insurance options, register with the public healthcare system (if eligible), and have a clear understanding of how you'll access healthcare services in Greece.

Learning the Greek Language and Culture

While many Greeks, especially in urban areas and tourist destinations, speak English, learning the Greek language will enhance your experience and integration into Greek society. Greek is a rich language with a unique alphabet, and even basic knowledge can go a long way in fostering connections with locals and navigating daily life.

Consider enrolling in a Greek language course either before your move or shortly after your arrival. Language schools and online resources are available to help you acquire the necessary language skills. Learning the language not only facilitates communication but also shows respect for the local culture.

Understanding Greek culture is equally important. Greeks take great pride in their traditions, festivals, and way of life. Engage with local customs, attend cultural events, and embrace the Mediterranean lifestyle. Whether it's joining in traditional dances at a village festival or participating in a religious procession, immersing yourself in Greek culture will enrich your experience and help you connect with the local community.

Conclusion

Preparing for your Greek adventure involves navigating legal requirements, financial planning, healthcare considerations, and cultural immersion. It's a multifaceted process that requires careful research and preparation, but it's a vital step in ensuring a successful and fulfilling relocation to Greece.

In the following chapters, we'll explore specific aspects of living in Greece in greater detail, from choosing your destination and finding accommodation to employment opportunities and education options. Each step you take brings you closer to realizing your dream of living in this beautiful Mediterranean country.

As you embark on this journey of preparation, keep in mind that moving to Greece is not just about changing your location; it's about embracing a new way of life, experiencing a different culture, and forging your path in a land rich in history and natural beauty.

Kalí týchi! (Good luck!)

Choosing Your Greek Destination

Greece, with its diverse geography and myriad of islands and regions, offers a wealth of choices when it comes to selecting your ideal destination. The country's different areas each have their unique charm, lifestyle, and appeal. Whether you're drawn to the vibrant urban energy of Athens, the idyllic shores of the Greek islands, or the tranquil villages of the mainland, this chapter will help you explore the options and make an informed decision about where to move in Greece.

Overview of Greece's Regions

Greece is divided into several distinct regions, each offering its unique character and attractions. Here's a brief overview of some of the key regions to consider:

1. **Attica (Athens)**: The capital city of Athens is the cultural and economic heart of Greece. It offers a bustling urban lifestyle with world-class museums, historical sites, and vibrant neighborhoods. Living in Athens provides access to a wide range of amenities, but it can also be fast-paced and cosmopolitan.
2. **Peloponnese**: The Peloponnese, a large peninsula in southern Greece, is known for its historical significance and natural beauty. Cities like Nafplio and Kalamata offer a blend of history and coastal living, while the region's inland areas are rich in archaeological sites.
3. **Central Greece**: This region includes cities like Larissa and Volos and is known for its agricultural production and beautiful landscapes. It's a more relaxed and traditional part of Greece, perfect for those seeking a slower pace of life.
4. **Thessaloniki and Northern Greece**: Thessaloniki, Greece's second-largest city, is the cultural hub of northern Greece. It boasts a lively arts scene, a historic waterfront, and a more

relaxed atmosphere compared to Athens.
5. **Crete**: The largest Greek island, Crete, offers a diverse range of experiences. You can choose between the bustling city life of Heraklion or Chania, or the tranquil villages in the countryside. Crete is known for its unique culture and stunning beaches.
6. **Cyclades**: This group of islands in the central Aegean Sea includes popular destinations like Mykonos and Santorini. The Cyclades are renowned for their beautiful beaches, vibrant nightlife, and traditional architecture.
7. **Ionian Islands**: Situated off the west coast of Greece, the Ionian Islands, including Corfu, Zakynthos, and Kefalonia, are known for their lush landscapes, turquoise waters, and a more relaxed pace of life.
8. **Aegean Islands**: Beyond the Cyclades, the Aegean Islands include Rhodes, Kos, and Samos. They offer a mix of historical sites, beaches, and picturesque villages.
9. **Epirus**: This region in northwestern Greece is known for its mountainous terrain and outdoor activities like hiking and rafting. It's a quieter and less touristy area, perfect for nature enthusiasts.
10. **Thessaly**: Located in central Greece, Thessaly is characterized by its vast plains and the stunning Meteora rock formations. It's a unique destination for those seeking tranquility and natural beauty.

Popular Expat Destinations

While Greece has a variety of appealing destinations, certain areas have become particularly popular among expats. These destinations often offer a good balance of amenities, community, and quality of life. Here are some of the top choices:

1. **Athens**: The capital city attracts expats seeking a dynamic

urban lifestyle, career opportunities, and access to cultural events. The neighborhoods of Kolonaki, Kifisia, and Glyfada are popular among the international community.
2. **Thessaloniki**: Greece's second-largest city, Thessaloniki, is known for its vibrant arts scene and thriving expat community. It offers a cosmopolitan atmosphere with a more relaxed pace of life compared to Athens.
3. **Crete**: Crete is a diverse island that appeals to a wide range of expats. Heraklion, Chania, and Rethymno are popular cities, each offering its unique blend of history, culture, and coastal living.
4. **Corfu**: This Ionian island is famous for its lush landscapes and beautiful beaches. The town of Corfu is a popular destination for expats, offering a mix of amenities and a charming old town.
5. **Santorini**: Although often associated with tourism, Santorini has attracted expats looking for a unique lifestyle. The island offers stunning views, a relaxed pace of life, and opportunities in tourism-related businesses.
6. **Kalamata**: Located in the Peloponnese, Kalamata is known for its Mediterranean climate, beautiful beaches, and affordable living. It's an excellent choice for expats seeking a more relaxed lifestyle.
7. **Rhodes**: Rhodes, in the Dodecanese group of islands, offers a mix of historical sites and coastal living. The city of Rhodes is a popular destination for expats, providing a range of amenities.

Climate, Lifestyle, and Local Amenities

When choosing your Greek destination, consider the climate, lifestyle, and available amenities, as these factors can significantly impact your quality of life.

1. **Climate**: Greece enjoys a Mediterranean climate, characterized

by hot, dry summers and mild, wet winters. The islands generally have milder winters than the mainland. Consider your preference for weather when selecting your destination.
2. **Lifestyle**: Greece offers a diverse range of lifestyles. Urban centers like Athens and Thessaloniki provide access to cultural events, career opportunities, and a vibrant social scene. Islands and smaller towns may offer a quieter, more relaxed way of life.
3. **Local Amenities**: Consider the availability of essential amenities like healthcare facilities, schools, and grocery stores. Major cities typically offer a broader range of services, while rural areas may have fewer options.
4. **Community**: The expat community varies by destination. In larger cities and popular expat areas, you're more likely to find an established expat network. Research local community groups and forums to connect with fellow expats.
5. **Accessibility**: Greece's geographical location makes it easy to explore neighboring countries and regions. Consider the proximity of your chosen destination to airports, ports, and major transportation hubs for travel convenience.

Ultimately, the right Greek destination for you will align with your lifestyle preferences, career goals, and personal interests. Take the time to explore different areas, conduct research, and even visit potential destinations to get a feel for what suits you best.

Conclusion

Choosing your Greek destination is a pivotal step in your journey to relocating to this enchanting Mediterranean country. Greece's diverse regions and islands offer a range of lifestyles, from the urban energy of Athens to the serene beauty of the islands and countryside.

Consider factors such as climate, lifestyle, local amenities, and community when making your decision. Each destination has its unique charm, and finding the one that resonates with your goals and preferences will set the stage for a rewarding Greek adventure.

In the chapters that follow, we'll delve deeper into the practical aspects of living in Greece, from finding your ideal home to navigating the bureaucracy and adapting to the local culture. Your chosen destination will play a significant role in shaping your experience, so choose wisely, and let the beauty and richness of Greece enrich your life.

Kalí týchi! (Good luck!)

Finding Your Greek Home

Finding the perfect home in Greece is a significant step in your journey to becoming a resident of this beautiful Mediterranean country. Whether you're seeking a modern apartment in Athens, a traditional village house on an island, or a countryside villa on the mainland, Greece offers a wide range of housing options to suit various lifestyles and preferences. In this chapter, we'll explore the process of finding your Greek home and the factors to consider when making this important decision.

Understanding the Greek Property Market

Before diving into your search for a Greek home, it's essential to gain an understanding of the country's property market. The Greek real estate market has experienced fluctuations over the years, influenced by economic conditions, tourism trends, and legal changes.

Here are some key points to keep in mind:

1. **Property Types**: Greece offers various types of properties, including apartments, houses, villas, and even historic buildings like stone houses. Each property type has its unique advantages and considerations.
2. **Property Prices**: Property prices in Greece vary significantly depending on location. Major cities and popular tourist destinations tend to have higher property prices, while rural areas and some islands may offer more affordable options.
3. **Market Trends**: Stay informed about current market trends and conditions. Economic factors, such as currency exchange rates and local economic stability, can impact property prices and availability.
4. **Legal Considerations**: Familiarize yourself with Greek property laws and regulations, especially if you're not an EU citizen. Legal requirements for property ownership and residency permits can differ based on your nationality.

5. **Local Market Differences**: Greece's property market can differ from one region to another. What's typical in Athens may not be the norm in a small village on an island. Local real estate agents can provide valuable insights.

Choosing Your Location

The location of your future home is one of the most critical decisions you'll make. Greece offers diverse regions, each with its unique charm and lifestyle. Here are some factors to consider when choosing your location:

1. **Proximity to Amenities**: Think about your daily needs, such as access to grocery stores, healthcare facilities, schools, and transportation. Decide whether you prefer a rural, suburban, or urban setting.
2. **Climate**: Greece's climate varies by region. Consider whether you prefer a coastal area with milder winters or are open to experiencing all four seasons in the mainland.
3. **Community and Lifestyle**: Explore the local culture, community, and lifestyle of potential destinations. Each area offers a distinct way of life, from bustling city living to tranquil village life.
4. **Accessibility**: Think about how accessible your chosen location is. Consider proximity to airports, ports, and major highways for travel and convenience.
5. **Scenic Beauty**: Greece is renowned for its natural beauty. Do you prefer coastal views, mountain landscapes, or lush countryside? The scenery can significantly impact your daily life and overall experience.
6. **Budget**: Your budget may influence your choice of location. While some areas are more affordable than others, keep in mind that property prices can vary widely even within the same region.

7. **Community and Expat Network**: Research the expat community and local amenities available in your chosen location. Access to services, social opportunities, and a support network can enhance your experience.

Working with Real Estate Agents

Navigating the Greek property market can be complex, especially if you're not familiar with local regulations and practices. Enlisting the services of a reputable real estate agent can be invaluable. Here's how to work effectively with a real estate agent in Greece:

1. **Choose a Local Agent**: Opt for a local real estate agent with a strong presence in your desired area. Local agents have in-depth knowledge of the market, properties, and legal requirements.
2. **Define Your Requirements**: Clearly communicate your property requirements and budget to your agent. This includes the type of property, number of bedrooms, amenities, and any specific features you desire.
3. **Set Realistic Expectations**: Be prepared to adjust your expectations based on the local market conditions. What's available and affordable in one location may differ from another.
4. **Legal Expertise**: Ensure your agent is well-versed in Greek property laws and regulations, especially if you're an international buyer. They should be able to guide you through the legal process.
5. **Visit Properties**: Whenever possible, visit properties in person to get a feel for the neighborhood and condition of the property. If you can't be there in person, ask for virtual tours or detailed photos.
6. **Negotiate Wisely**: Real estate transactions in Greece often involve negotiation. Trust your agent's guidance on making

competitive offers and negotiating terms.
7. **Due Diligence**: Conduct due diligence on any property you're interested in. This includes inspections, surveys, and reviewing the property's legal status.

Property Ownership and Legal Considerations

Understanding the legal aspects of property ownership in Greece is crucial for a smooth and secure purchase. Here are some key legal considerations:

1. **Ownership Restrictions**: Non-EU citizens may have restrictions on owning property in Greece. Consult with legal experts to understand the specific regulations and requirements.
2. **Title Deeds**: Ensure that the property you're interested in has clear and legal title deeds. Your lawyer can help verify the property's ownership history and any encumbrances.
3. **Legal Representation**: Hiring a Greek attorney with expertise in property law is highly advisable. They will guide you through the legal process, assist with contracts, and conduct necessary checks.
4. **Property Taxes**: Be aware of property taxes in Greece, including annual property tax (ENFIA) and any local taxes. Your lawyer can provide details on tax obligations.
5. **Notary and Registration**: Property transactions in Greece require the presence of a notary public. They oversee the contract signing and registration process to ensure the legality of the transaction.

Financing Your Property Purchase

If you're planning to finance your property purchase, it's essential to explore your options and understand the financing process in Greece:

1. **Mortgages**: Greek banks offer mortgage loans to both residents and non-residents. However, lending criteria, interest rates, and loan terms can vary, so shop around for the best deal.
2. **Deposit Requirements**: Be prepared to provide a significant down payment, typically ranging from 20% to 40% of the property's purchase price.
3. **Currency Exchange**: Consider the currency exchange rate, as your loan may be in euros, even if your income is in another currency. Exchange rate fluctuations can impact your loan repayments.
4. **Bank Requirements**: Greek banks may require extensive documentation, including proof of income, residency status, and credit history, to approve a mortgage.
5. **Legal Assistance**: Engage with legal professionals who can review the terms of your mortgage agreement and ensure you understand your financial obligations.

Property Inspection and Evaluation

Before finalizing your property purchase, it's essential to conduct a thorough inspection and evaluation. Here's what you should consider:

1. **Property Inspection**: Hire a qualified property inspector to assess the condition of the property. They can identify any structural issues, necessary repairs, or maintenance requirements.
2. **Appraisal**: Consider obtaining a professional property appraisal to determine the property's fair market value. This can help you negotiate a reasonable purchase price.
3. **Legal Documentation**: Review all legal documents related to the property, including contracts, title deeds, and any permits or licenses. Ensure everything is in order before proceeding.
4. **Utilities and Services**: Verify the availability and functionality of essential utilities and services, such as water, electricity,

heating, and internet connectivity.
5. **Survey and Boundaries**: Conduct a property survey to define the boundaries and any potential encroachments. Ensure that the property size matches the information provided.
6. **Environmental Considerations**: Inquire about any potential environmental concerns, such as flood zones or protected areas that could affect your property.

The Purchase Process

Once you've identified your ideal property, completed due diligence, and secured financing, you can move forward with the purchase process. Here's an overview of the steps involved:

1. **Reservation Agreement**: In some cases, you may need to sign a reservation agreement and provide a deposit to secure the property while the legal and financial details are finalized.
2. **Contract of Sale**: The contract of sale outlines the terms and conditions of the property purchase, including the purchase price, payment schedule, and expected closing date. Your attorney will review and negotiate the contract on your behalf.
3. **Notary Public**: The contract signing typically takes place in the presence of a notary public, who ensures the legality of the transaction and registers it with the Land Registry.
4. **Transfer Tax and Fees**: Be prepared to pay transfer tax, notary fees, and other associated costs at the time of the property transfer.
5. **Final Inspection**: Prior to the property transfer, conduct a final inspection to ensure it meets the agreed-upon conditions and is in the expected condition.
6. **Property Transfer**: The property transfer involves the legal transfer of ownership from the seller to the buyer. This is completed at the Land Registry office.
7. **Utilities and Services**: Transfer utility and service accounts to

your name, including water, electricity, and internet.
8. **Property Insurance**: Consider purchasing property insurance to protect your investment against unforeseen events.

Conclusion

Finding your Greek home is a significant milestone in your journey to living in Greece. By understanding the property market, choosing the right location, working with experienced professionals, and navigating the legal aspects of property ownership, you can secure a comfortable and fulfilling place to call home.

Your Greek home will not only be a place to reside but also a gateway to experiencing the rich culture, stunning landscapes, and warm hospitality that Greece has to offer. In the upcoming chapters, we'll explore other essential aspects of life in Greece, from employment opportunities and education to healthcare and integration into the local community.

As you embark on this exciting chapter of your life, may your new Greek home be a source of joy, comfort, and countless memorable moments in this enchanting Mediterranean paradise.

Kalí týchi! (Good luck!)

Navigating Greek Bureaucracy

Navigating bureaucracy is a necessary part of relocating to any country, and Greece is no exception. While the country offers a warm Mediterranean welcome, its administrative processes can be intricate and time-consuming. In this chapter, we'll guide you through the essential steps and considerations for dealing with Greek bureaucracy, from obtaining residence permits to setting up utilities and handling legal matters.

Residence Permits and Visas

For non-EU citizens planning to reside in Greece, obtaining the necessary residence permit is a crucial step. The type of permit you need depends on your reason for moving to Greece, such as employment, retirement, or family reunification. Here's an overview of the residence permit process:

1. **Entry Visa**: If required based on your nationality, obtain an entry visa for Greece before your arrival. This visa allows you to enter the country and begin the residence permit application process.
2. **Residence Permit Categories**: Greece offers various residence permit categories, including work permits, family reunification permits, and retirement permits. Ensure you apply for the appropriate category based on your circumstances.
3. **Documentation**: Prepare the required documents, which typically include a valid passport, proof of income, health insurance, and a clean criminal record. Check with the Greek consulate or embassy in your home country for the specific documents needed for your permit type.
4. **Application Submission**: Submit your residence permit application to the relevant authorities in Greece, such as the Greek Immigration Office (Alien's Bureau). You may need to schedule an appointment or visit the office in person.

A GUIDE TO RELOCATING TO GREECE

5. **Biometric Data**: Provide biometric data, such as fingerprints and a photograph, as part of the application process.
6. **Processing Time**: Residence permit processing times can vary. Be prepared for potential delays and follow up with the authorities on the status of your application.
7. **Legal Assistance**: Consider enlisting the services of a Greek attorney experienced in immigration and residency matters. They can guide you through the process, help with documentation, and assist with any appeals if needed.

Taxation and Financial Matters

Understanding the Greek tax system and fulfilling your financial obligations is essential for legal compliance. Here are some key considerations:

1. **Tax Identification Number (AFM)**: You'll need to obtain a Greek Tax Identification Number (AFM) for various financial transactions, including employment, property ownership, and opening a bank account.
2. **Income Tax**: Greece has a progressive income tax system. Be aware of your tax obligations and ensure you file your income tax return annually. Non-residents may have different tax rates and rules.
3. **Property Taxes**: Property owners in Greece are subject to property taxes, including the annual property tax known as ENFIA. Stay informed about property tax rates and deadlines.
4. **Banking and Accounts**: Open a local bank account in Greece to facilitate financial transactions. Greek banks may require proof of residence and a tax identification number.
5. **Currency Exchange**: Be mindful of currency exchange rates if you're receiving income or holding assets in a foreign currency. Exchange rate fluctuations can impact your financial situation.
6. **Financial Advisors**: Consult with financial advisors or tax

professionals who specialize in Greek taxation to ensure compliance and optimize your financial planning.

Utilities and Services

Setting up essential utilities and services in Greece is a practical aspect of your relocation. Here's how to manage the process:

1. **Water and Electricity**: Contact the local water and electricity providers to have utilities connected in your name. You may need to provide identification and proof of residence.
2. **Internet and Phone**: Choose an internet and phone service provider and select a plan that suits your needs. Installation may require an appointment and proof of residence.
3. **Heating and Cooling**: If your property includes heating or cooling systems, ensure they are in working order. Heating options can vary, from central heating to air conditioning units.
4. **Trash and Recycling**: Learn about local waste disposal and recycling procedures. In many areas, you'll need to separate your trash and adhere to specific collection schedules.
5. **Postal Services**: Set up a postal address and check the local post office for mail delivery options. Post office services can vary by region.

Healthcare and Insurance

Access to healthcare and appropriate insurance coverage is a vital aspect of your relocation to Greece:

1. **Public Healthcare**: Greece has a public healthcare system known as the National Healthcare System (EOPYY). EU citizens may be eligible for free or reduced-cost healthcare services by registering with EOPYY.
2. **Private Health Insurance**: Many residents opt for private

health insurance to access a broader range of healthcare facilities and services. Research insurance providers and select a plan that meets your needs.
3. **Pharmacies**: Familiarize yourself with the location of pharmacies in your area. Pharmacies in Greece are abundant and provide both prescription and over-the-counter medications.
4. **Medical Facilities**: Identify the nearest medical facilities, clinics, and hospitals in your vicinity for emergency and routine healthcare needs.

Legal Matters and Notary Services

Legal considerations are an integral part of navigating Greek bureaucracy:

1. **Notary Services**: Notaries in Greece oversee various legal processes, including property transactions, contracts, and powers of attorney. Engage with a reputable notary public for any legal documentation needs.
2. **Legal Representation**: Consider hiring a Greek attorney with expertise in immigration, property law, or any other legal matters relevant to your situation. They can provide guidance and representation when necessary.
3. **Translations**: Some official documents may require translation into Greek by a certified translator. Ensure that translations are accurate and meet the requirements of Greek authorities.

Vehicle and Driver's License

If you plan to drive in Greece, whether with your own vehicle or a rental, be aware of the following:

1. **Driver's License**: If you hold a valid EU or EEA driver's license, you can use it in Greece without the need for an

international driver's permit (IDP). Non-EU/EEA citizens may need an IDP.
2. **Vehicle Registration**: If you plan to bring your vehicle to Greece, you'll need to register it with the local authorities. Consider consulting with a customs broker or transportation expert for guidance.
3. **Insurance**: Ensure that you have adequate insurance coverage for your vehicle. Greek law requires third-party liability insurance.
4. **Road Rules**: Familiarize yourself with Greek road rules and regulations, including speed limits, parking restrictions, and tolls.

Community Integration and Networking

As you navigate Greek bureaucracy, building connections within your local community and with fellow expats can be valuable:

1. **Expat Groups**: Join local expat groups and online communities to connect with others who have experienced similar challenges and can provide guidance.
2. **Local Events**: Participate in local events, festivals, and cultural activities to immerse yourself in Greek life and build relationships with neighbors and residents.
3. **Language Learning**: Invest time in learning the Greek language. Even basic knowledge can enhance your interactions and integration into the community.

Conclusion

Navigating Greek bureaucracy may seem daunting at times, but with patience, preparation, and a proactive approach, you can successfully handle administrative processes and requirements. Seek assistance from experienced professionals, follow legal guidelines, and build a support network within your local community and among fellow expats.

Remember that the effort you put into understanding and managing Greek bureaucracy is an essential part of your journey to fully embracing the Greek way of life. As you overcome administrative challenges, you'll be better equipped to enjoy the rich culture, stunning landscapes, and warm hospitality that Greece has to offer.

Kalí týchi! (Good luck!)

Employment and Entrepreneurship in Greece

Securing employment or pursuing entrepreneurship opportunities in Greece can be a rewarding venture, offering a chance to immerse yourself in the country's rich culture while contributing to its economic landscape. In this chapter, we'll explore the job market, employment opportunities, and the process of starting a business in Greece.

Understanding the Greek Job Market

Before seeking employment in Greece, it's crucial to understand the country's job market dynamics, economic conditions, and employment trends:

1. **Economic Situation**: Greece has experienced economic challenges in recent years, leading to fluctuations in the job market. However, there are signs of recovery and growth in various sectors.
2. **Job Opportunities**: Employment opportunities can vary by industry and region. The tourism and hospitality sector is a significant source of jobs, especially in popular tourist destinations. Other sectors include shipping, agriculture, manufacturing, and technology.
3. **Language Skills**: Proficiency in the Greek language can significantly impact your job prospects. While some international companies and roles may require English, many local positions necessitate Greek fluency.
4. **Networking**: Building a professional network in Greece is essential. Personal connections often play a crucial role in accessing job openings and opportunities.
5. **Recruitment Agencies**: Consider working with recruitment agencies that specialize in your industry. They can help match your skills and qualifications with suitable job openings.

A GUIDE TO RELOCATING TO GREECE

6. **Freelancing and Remote Work**: Freelancing and remote work opportunities are becoming increasingly common in Greece, especially in fields such as digital marketing, web development, and content creation.

Finding Employment in Greece

When searching for employment in Greece, consider the following steps:

1. **Job Search**: Explore job search platforms, both online and in print, such as LinkedIn, local job websites, and newspaper classifieds. Additionally, network with professionals in your field and attend industry events.
2. **CV and Cover Letter**: Prepare a well-structured curriculum vitae (CV) and a tailored cover letter for each job application. Highlight relevant skills and experience, and emphasize your commitment to living and working in Greece.
3. **Interview Preparation**: Practice for interviews, and be ready to discuss your qualifications, experience, and your motivation to work in Greece. Familiarize yourself with common interview questions and cultural norms.
4. **Work Permits**: Ensure that you have the necessary work permit and residence permit, if applicable, before accepting a job offer. Employers may assist with the permit process.
5. **Local Hiring Practices**: Understand local hiring practices, including the importance of personal connections and recommendations. Networking within your industry can open doors to job opportunities.
6. **Employment Contracts**: Carefully review and understand your employment contract, including terms, conditions, and benefits. Seek legal advice if needed.
7. **Professional Development**: Stay updated with industry trends and consider investing in additional training or certifications to

enhance your qualifications.

Entrepreneurship and Business Opportunities

If you're considering entrepreneurship in Greece, the country offers various opportunities and incentives for starting and running a business:

1. **Business Climate**: Greece is working to improve its business climate, with reforms aimed at simplifying administrative procedures and reducing bureaucracy.
2. **Start-Up Ecosystem**: Major cities like Athens and Thessaloniki have burgeoning start-up ecosystems, with co-working spaces, incubators, and support networks for entrepreneurs.
3. **Business Sectors**: Explore sectors with growth potential in Greece, such as tourism, agribusiness, renewable energy, technology, and e-commerce.
4. **Start-Up Programs**: Look for government-supported start-up programs and grants that provide financial incentives and support for new businesses.
5. **Legal Structure**: Choose an appropriate legal structure for your business, such as a sole proprietorship, limited liability company, or partnership. Seek legal advice to ensure compliance with Greek business laws.
6. **Business Plan**: Develop a comprehensive business plan that outlines your business concept, target market, financial projections, and marketing strategy. A well-structured plan can attract investors and lenders.
7. **Funding and Financing**: Explore funding options, including venture capital, angel investors, crowdfunding, and business loans from banks and financial institutions.
8. **Regulatory Compliance**: Be aware of regulatory requirements, including business registration, tax obligations, and licenses or permits, depending on your industry.

Starting a Business in Greece

Starting a business in Greece involves several steps, including:

1. **Business Idea and Plan**: Begin by formulating a clear business idea and creating a detailed business plan.
2. **Legal Structure**: Choose a legal structure for your business, such as a sole proprietorship, partnership, limited liability company, or corporation.
3. **Company Registration**: Register your business with the Greek General Commercial Registry (GEMI). This involves selecting a unique business name and submitting the necessary documents, including your business plan and financial statements.
4. **Tax Registration**: Obtain a Greek Tax Identification Number (AFM) for your business. This will be required for tax purposes and financial transactions.
5. **Bank Account**: Open a business bank account to manage your finances and transactions.
6. **Licenses and Permits**: Depending on your industry and location, you may need specific licenses or permits to operate legally. Research and apply for any necessary permits.
7. **Accounting and Taxes**: Set up an accounting system to keep track of your business finances. Comply with Greek tax regulations, including VAT (Value Added Tax) and income tax.
8. **Employment and Labor**: If you plan to hire employees, familiarize yourself with Greek labor laws and employment regulations. Register your employees with social security and provide appropriate benefits.
9. **Insurance**: Consider insurance coverage for your business, including liability insurance and coverage for assets and inventory.

10. **Marketing and Promotion**: Develop a marketing strategy to promote your business locally and, if applicable, internationally.
11. **Network and Collaborate**: Join business associations, chambers of commerce, and industry-specific organizations to network and collaborate with other entrepreneurs.

Challenges and Considerations

While Greece offers opportunities for employment and entrepreneurship, it's important to be aware of the challenges and considerations:

1. **Economic Factors**: Greece has faced economic challenges, including high unemployment rates. It may take time to secure stable employment or establish a successful business.
2. **Language**: Proficiency in the Greek language is often required for many job opportunities and essential for conducting business effectively.
3. **Bureaucracy**: Greece has a reputation for bureaucratic processes, which can be time-consuming and complex. Be prepared for administrative hurdles when starting a business.
4. **Market Competition**: Some sectors may be highly competitive, requiring thorough market research and a unique value proposition to succeed.
5. **Legal and Taxation**: Greek business laws and tax regulations may differ from those in your home country. Seek legal and financial advice to ensure compliance.
6. **Cultural Adaptation**: Adapting to Greek business culture and customs may require patience and flexibility.

Conclusion

Employment and entrepreneurship opportunities in Greece can be fulfilling and enriching experiences. Whether you choose to pursue a career in an existing industry, explore entrepreneurial ventures, or combine both paths, thorough research, preparation, and a commitment to building connections within the local community will contribute to your success.

As you embark on your professional journey in Greece, remember to remain adaptable, embrace new experiences, and leverage the vibrant culture and dynamic business environment that Greece has to offer. Your contribution to the Greek workforce or business landscape can be a rewarding endeavor that allows you to be part of this Mediterranean country's continued growth and development.

Kalí týchi! (Good luck!)

Education and Schools

Providing your children with a quality education is a top priority when moving to a new country, and Greece offers a range of educational opportunities for expatriate families. This chapter will guide you through the Greek education system, including options for international and public schools, enrollment procedures, and considerations for your child's academic journey in Greece.

The Greek Education System

Understanding the structure of the Greek education system is essential for choosing the right educational path for your child. The Greek education system is divided into several levels:

1. **Preschool Education (Nipiagogeia)**: Preschool education is for children aged 2.5 to 5 years old and is not compulsory. It prepares children for primary school and focuses on socialization and basic skills.
2. **Primary Education (Dimotiko)**: Primary education is compulsory for children aged 6 to 12 years old. It consists of six grades and covers a broad curriculum, including Greek language, mathematics, science, art, and physical education.
3. **Lower Secondary Education (Gymnasio)**: After completing primary school, students attend the lower secondary education level, which includes three grades (7th, 8th, and 9th). The curriculum becomes more specialized, including subjects like history, geography, and foreign languages.
4. **Upper Secondary Education (Lykeio)**: Upper secondary education is for students aged 15 to 18 and lasts three years (10th, 11th, and 12th grades). Students choose a specific track (academic or vocational) that determines their curriculum. At the end of the lykeio, students take the Panhellenic Examinations (university entrance exams) to pursue higher

education.

International Schools in Greece

Expatriate families often choose international schools in Greece to provide their children with an education in their native language or an internationally recognized curriculum. Here are some popular international schools in Greece:

1. **American Community Schools of Athens (ACS Athens)**: ACS Athens offers an American-style education with English as the primary language of instruction. The school follows the American curriculum and provides students with the opportunity to earn a U.S. high school diploma.
2. **International School of Athens (ISA)**: ISA offers an international education with a focus on the International Baccalaureate (IB) program. The school follows the IB Primary Years Program (PYP), Middle Years Program (MYP), and Diploma Program (DP).
3. **Campus International School (CIS)**: CIS follows the Cambridge International Curriculum and offers instruction in English. The school provides Cambridge International Examinations and prepares students for IGCSE (International General Certificate of Secondary Education) and A-level examinations.
4. **Costeas-Geitonas School**: This school offers a Greek and International Baccalaureate (IB) curriculum, making it suitable for both Greek and international students. Instruction is in Greek and English.
5. **St. Catherine's British School**: St. Catherine's follows the British curriculum and offers IGCSE and A-level qualifications. English is the primary language of instruction.
6. **Deutsche Schule Athen (German School of Athens)**: For German-speaking families, this school follows the German

curriculum and offers the German International Abitur.

Public Schools in Greece

Public schools in Greece provide education to Greek students and may offer limited opportunities for non-Greek-speaking expatriates. While attending a public school can provide a cultural immersion experience, it may present challenges for non-Greek-speaking students. Here are some considerations for enrolling your child in a Greek public school:

1. **Language Barrier**: Greek is the primary language of instruction in public schools. Non-Greek-speaking students may face language barriers, especially in the early grades.
2. **Integration**: Public schools in Greece aim to integrate expatriate students into the Greek education system. Specialized language support and Greek as a Second Language (GSL) classes are often available.
3. **Curriculum**: The Greek curriculum may differ significantly from curricula in other countries. Research the curriculum to ensure it aligns with your educational goals for your child.
4. **Extracurricular Activities**: Public schools may offer extracurricular activities and cultural experiences that can enrich your child's education.
5. **Regional Variations**: The quality of public education in Greece can vary by region. Consider the location of your residence when evaluating public school options.

Enrollment Procedures

The enrollment process for schools in Greece varies depending on the type of school and the educational level. Here are general steps to enroll your child in a school in Greece:

1. **Residence**: Ensure that you have legal residence status in

Greece, as this may be required for school enrollment.
2. **Choose a School**: Research and select a school that meets your child's educational needs and preferences.
3. **Contact the School**: Reach out to the chosen school to inquire about the enrollment process, requirements, and available spaces.
4. **Documentation**: Prepare the necessary documents, which typically include your child's birth certificate, vaccination records, passport or identity card, residence permit, and any academic transcripts or certificates.
5. **Language Assessment**: If enrolling in a Greek school, your child may undergo a language assessment to determine their proficiency in Greek. Depending on the results, they may receive additional language support.
6. **Admissions Interview**: Some international schools may require an admissions interview or entrance exam, especially for older students.
7. **Registration**: Complete the school's registration forms and provide all required documentation.
8. **Tuition and Fees**: Be aware of tuition fees and payment schedules, which can vary widely among schools. Some international schools offer scholarships or financial aid.
9. **Orientation**: Attend orientation sessions or meetings with school staff to familiarize yourself and your child with the school's policies and procedures.
10. **Transportation**: Arrange transportation to and from the school, whether by school bus or other means.

Extracurricular Activities and Support

Many schools in Greece, both international and public, offer extracurricular activities, sports programs, and academic support services.

These activities can enhance your child's educational experience and provide opportunities to socialize and make friends.

Additionally, schools often have support services for students with special needs or learning differences. If your child requires such support, communicate with the school to ensure they receive the assistance they need to succeed academically.

Home Schooling

Home schooling is an option for families who prefer to educate their children independently or follow a specific curriculum not offered by traditional schools. If you choose home schooling in Greece, you must follow Greek regulations and requirements, including submitting an annual educational plan to the Ministry of Education and Religious Affairs.

Conclusion

Education is a significant consideration for expatriate families moving to Greece. Whether you opt for an international school, a public school, or home schooling, it's essential to choose the educational path that aligns with your child's needs and goals.

Keep in mind that the Greek education system places a strong emphasis on language proficiency in Greek, so language acquisition will be a crucial aspect of your child's education if they are not already fluent. By thoroughly researching your options, understanding the enrollment process, and engaging with school communities, you can provide your child with a meaningful and enriching educational experience in Greece.

Kalí týchi! (Good luck!)

Embracing Greek Culture

Embracing Greek culture is an essential aspect of your journey when moving to Greece. The country's rich history, traditions, cuisine, and way of life offer a unique and rewarding experience. In this chapter, we'll explore the many facets of Greek culture and provide insights into how you can immerse yourself in this vibrant Mediterranean lifestyle.

Cultural Diversity in Greece

Greece's culture is a blend of ancient traditions, modern influences, and regional diversity. Understanding this diversity can enhance your cultural immersion experience:

1. **Mainland vs. Islands**: Greece's mainland and its numerous islands each have their own distinct cultural characteristics. Coastal regions often have a more relaxed, islander mentality, while urban areas are influenced by contemporary European culture.
2. **Festivals and Celebrations**: Greece boasts a calendar full of festivals and celebrations, many of which are region-specific. From the lively Carnival celebrations in Patras to the religious processions of Easter in Corfu, participating in local festivities can offer a glimpse into regional customs.
3. **Cuisine**: Greek cuisine is celebrated worldwide for its Mediterranean flavors and ingredients. However, regional specialties and variations exist, so be sure to explore local dishes unique to your area.
4. **Dialects**: Greek is the official language, but dialects and regional accents differ across the country. Learning a bit of the local dialect can be a fun way to connect with residents.

Greek Hospitality (Philoxenia)

Greek hospitality, known as "philoxenia," is a cornerstone of Greek culture. It reflects the warmth, generosity, and friendliness of the Greek people. When you experience philoxenia, you'll find that:

1. **Invitations Are Common**: Greeks often extend invitations to their homes or for a meal. Accepting such invitations is a way to build relationships and experience traditional Greek hospitality.
2. **Sharing Food**: Sharing a meal is a fundamental aspect of Greek culture. Guests are offered the best food available, and it's customary to try a bit of everything served.
3. **Coffee Culture**: Greek coffee culture is a social activity. Cafes are gathering places where friends meet to chat, enjoy coffee, and play tavli (backgammon).
4. **Gift Giving**: It's customary to bring a small gift when invited to someone's home, such as flowers, wine, or dessert.

Greek Traditions and Customs

Greek traditions are deeply rooted in history and continue to be an integral part of daily life:

1. **Religious Celebrations**: Greek Orthodox Christianity plays a significant role in Greek culture. Religious celebrations, such as Easter and the Feast of the Assumption, are observed with great devotion and elaborate rituals.
2. **Name Days**: Name days are more important than birthdays in Greece. Each day is dedicated to a specific saint, and people celebrate their name day by hosting gatherings and receiving guests.
3. **Superstitions**: Greeks have a range of superstitions, such as the belief in the "evil eye." Protective charms and gestures like spitting are used to ward off bad luck.
4. **Dances and Music**: Traditional Greek dances, like the syrtaki

and zeibekiko, are an integral part of celebrations. Live music and dancing often accompany gatherings and events.

Cultural Immersion Activities

To fully embrace Greek culture, consider engaging in the following activities:

1. **Learn Greek**: Learning the Greek language is one of the most effective ways to immerse yourself in the culture. It allows you to communicate with locals more effectively and understand the nuances of daily life.
2. **Cooking Classes**: Take cooking classes to learn how to prepare traditional Greek dishes like moussaka, tzatziki, and baklava. Cooking and sharing meals with locals can be a bonding experience.
3. **Participate in Festivals**: Attend local festivals and celebrations to experience Greek music, dance, and traditions firsthand. Joining in the festivities is a great way to connect with the community.
4. **Explore Historical Sites**: Greece is rich in historical sites, including ancient ruins, monasteries, and archaeological museums. Exploring these sites provides insight into Greece's ancient heritage.
5. **Visit Local Markets**: Explore local markets, such as the bustling Varvakios Agora in Athens or the markets of Thessaloniki. These markets offer a glimpse into daily life and local products.
6. **Take Part in Religious Observances**: If you're comfortable, attend religious observances and services to witness the deep spirituality of Greek Orthodox Christianity.
7. **Participate in Social Activities**: Engage in social activities like dance classes, local sports, or arts and crafts workshops to connect with the community.

Cultural Sensitivity

While embracing Greek culture is encouraged, it's essential to be culturally sensitive and respectful:

1. **Dress Modestly**: When visiting churches or monasteries, dress modestly by covering shoulders and knees. This applies to both men and women.
2. **Respect Religious Customs**: During religious ceremonies, maintain a respectful demeanor and refrain from loud conversation or inappropriate behavior.
3. **Politeness**: Use polite language and observe social etiquette when interacting with locals, including using "please" and "thank you."
4. **Gift Giving**: When offering gifts, do so with your right hand or both hands. Using the left hand alone is considered impolite.

Conclusion

Embracing Greek culture is an enriching journey that will deepen your appreciation for this beautiful Mediterranean country. By immersing yourself in local traditions, participating in community events, and making an effort to connect with residents, you'll gain a profound understanding of Greece's rich history and vibrant way of life.

As you embrace Greek culture, you'll not only become a welcomed member of the community but also create lasting memories and friendships that will enhance your experience of living in this captivating country.

Kalí týchi! (Good luck!)

Exploring Greek Cuisine

Greek cuisine is a testament to the country's rich history, diverse landscapes, and Mediterranean climate. Characterized by fresh, locally sourced ingredients and robust flavors, Greek food is both delicious and deeply rooted in tradition. In this chapter, we will take a culinary journey through the flavors of Greece, from classic dishes to regional specialties, and provide tips on where to experience Greek cuisine at its finest.

The Mediterranean Diet

Greek cuisine is often celebrated for its adherence to the Mediterranean diet, which is renowned for its health benefits. Key aspects of the Mediterranean diet include:

1. **Olive Oil**: Olive oil is the cornerstone of Greek cooking. It's used for cooking, dressing salads, and drizzling over dishes, adding a distinctive flavor and healthy monounsaturated fats.
2. **Fresh Produce**: Greek cuisine emphasizes the use of fresh, seasonal fruits and vegetables, such as tomatoes, cucumbers, peppers, and eggplants. Greeks take pride in the quality of their produce.
3. **Whole Grains**: Whole grains like barley, bulgur, and rice are common in Greek dishes, providing a hearty and nutritious base for many meals.
4. **Lean Proteins**: Greek cuisine incorporates lean proteins, including fish, poultry, and legumes. Fish, especially in coastal regions, is a staple.
5. **Herbs and Spices**: Fresh herbs like oregano, basil, and mint, along with aromatic spices like cinnamon and cloves, infuse Greek dishes with flavor.
6. **Dairy**: Yogurt and feta cheese are prevalent in Greek cuisine, offering creamy textures and tangy flavors.
7. **Wine and Raki**: Greece is home to a thriving wine culture,

and the traditional spirit known as raki or tsipouro is often enjoyed as an aperitif or digestif.

Classic Greek Dishes

When exploring Greek cuisine, you'll encounter a variety of classic dishes that showcase the country's culinary heritage. Here are some iconic Greek dishes to savor:

1. **Moussaka**: A layered casserole of eggplant, minced meat (often lamb or beef), and béchamel sauce, baked to perfection. It's a comforting and hearty dish.
2. **Souvlaki**: Skewered and grilled pieces of marinated meat (usually pork, chicken, or lamb) served with pita bread, vegetables, and tzatziki sauce.
3. **Tzatziki**: A creamy yogurt-based dip or sauce with cucumber, garlic, and fresh dill, often served with grilled meats or as a dip for bread.
4. **Dolmades**: Grape leaves stuffed with a mixture of rice, herbs, and sometimes ground meat. They are typically served as an appetizer or side dish.
5. **Greek Salad (Horiatiki)**: A refreshing salad made with tomatoes, cucumbers, red onions, Kalamata olives, and feta cheese, drizzled with olive oil and sprinkled with oregano.
6. **Spanakopita**: A savory pastry filled with spinach, feta cheese, onions, and herbs, encased in flaky phyllo dough.
7. **Pastitsio**: A baked pasta dish similar to lasagna, with layers of pasta, seasoned meat, and béchamel sauce.
8. **Saganaki**: Fried cheese, typically Kasseri or feta, served with a splash of lemon juice and often flambéed with brandy at the table.
9. **Kleftiko**: Slow-cooked lamb or goat, marinated with garlic and herbs, then sealed in parchment paper or clay pots to trap the flavors.

10. **Octopus**: Grilled or stewed octopus, often served as a seafood appetizer or meze.

Regional Delicacies

Greece's regional diversity is reflected in its culinary traditions. Each region boasts its own specialties and flavors. Here are some regional delicacies to seek out:

1. **Crete**: Crete is known for its hearty and nutritious cuisine. Try "dakos," a salad made with barley rusks, tomatoes, and feta cheese, or "stifado," a flavorful stew with onions and rabbit or beef.
2. **Santorini**: This island is famous for its sun-dried tomatoes, white eggplants, and "santorinio," a tomato-based fish stew.
3. **Thessaloniki**: Greece's second-largest city is renowned for "bougatsa," a sweet pastry filled with custard or cheese, and "koulouri," a sesame seed-covered bread ring.
4. **Peloponnese**: In this region, indulge in "spetzofai," a dish of sausage and peppers cooked in a tomato sauce, or "pastelaki," a sweet sesame and honey bar.
5. **Naxos**: The island of Naxos is known for its "kitron," a liqueur made from citron leaves, and "potatoes of Naxos," a unique potato variety cultivated in the rich volcanic soil.

Seafood and Coastal Cuisine

Given Greece's extensive coastline, seafood features prominently in its cuisine. Fresh fish, octopus, squid, and shellfish are staples in coastal regions. Some coastal specialties to enjoy include:

1. **Grilled Fish**: Savory and aromatic, grilled whole fish, such as sea bream or red snapper, is a delight, often served with olive oil and lemon.
2. **Calamari**: Tender and crispy fried calamari, served with a

squeeze of lemon and often accompanied by tzatziki sauce.
3. **Gavros**: Marinated anchovies, served as a cold appetizer or meze, often paired with ouzo or raki.
4. **Lavraki**: Also known as bronzino or European sea bass, lavraki is a prized fish in Greek cuisine, prepared in various ways, including baked with herbs and lemon.

Desserts and Sweets

Greek desserts are a sweet ending to any meal, and they often incorporate honey, nuts, and phyllo dough. Some delectable options include:

1. **Baklava**: Layers of phyllo dough filled with chopped nuts, sweetened with syrup or honey, and flavored with cinnamon and cloves.
2. **Loukoumades**: Small, fried dough balls drizzled with honey and sprinkled with cinnamon, often served hot and crispy.
3. **Galaktoboureko**: A creamy custard dessert enclosed in phyllo pastry and soaked in syrup.
4. **Kourabiedes**: Butter cookies coated in powdered sugar and studded with almonds, often enjoyed during holidays and celebrations.
5. **Ravani**: A semolina cake soaked in syrup and often flavored with rosewater or orange blossom water.

Wine and Spirits

Greek wine has a long and storied history, with many indigenous grape varieties. Explore Greek wines, both red and white, from regions like Nemea, Naoussa, and Santorini. Additionally, try the traditional spirit known as raki (or tsipouro), which is often enjoyed as an aperitif or digestif.

Coffee Culture

Greek coffee culture is a cherished tradition. Coffeehouses (kafenia) are popular gathering spots for locals and visitors alike. Greek coffee is strong and served in small cups. You can order it sweet (glykós), semi-sweet (metri), or unsweetened (sketos). Enjoying a Greek coffee is an opportunity to relax and savor the moment.

Dining Etiquette

When dining in Greece, keep these dining etiquette tips in mind:

1. **Table Manners**: Place your napkin on your lap, and keep your hands visible above the table. It's polite to finish everything on your plate.
2. **Tipping**: Tipping is customary in Greece. A standard tip is around 10% to 15% of the bill. In tavernas, you may leave loose change as a tip.
3. **Reservations**: In popular restaurants, especially during the tourist season, it's advisable to make reservations.
4. **Dress Code**: Dress casually but neatly when dining in most restaurants. For upscale dining establishments, smart casual attire is appropriate.
5. **Smoking**: Smoking is prohibited in indoor dining areas, but it is allowed in outdoor seating areas in some places.
6. **Paying the Bill**: In Greece, it's common for the waiter to bring the bill only when requested. You can signal that you're ready to pay by making a "writing" gesture in the air.

Local Markets and Food Tours

Exploring local markets, such as the Central Market in Athens or the Varvakios Agora, is a sensory delight. You'll find fresh produce, spices, cheeses, and more. Additionally, consider joining a food tour led by a local guide who can introduce you to hidden gems and provide insights into the culinary traditions of the region.

Cooking Classes

Participating in a cooking class is an excellent way to learn the art of Greek cuisine. You'll have the opportunity to work with local ingredients, master traditional recipes, and gain valuable culinary skills to replicate the flavors of Greece at home.

Conclusion

Greek cuisine is a celebration of fresh ingredients, robust flavors, and culinary traditions that span millennia. Exploring Greek food is not just about savoring delicious dishes but also about immersing yourself in a cultural experience that reflects the heart and soul of Greece.

Whether you're indulging in classic dishes, savoring regional specialties, or enjoying the warm hospitality of a local taverna, Greek cuisine is sure to leave a lasting impression and create fond memories of your time in this Mediterranean paradise.

Kali orexi! (Bon appétit!)

Staying Safe and Healthy

Moving to Greece offers an opportunity for a vibrant and enriching life, but it's essential to prioritize your safety and well-being. This chapter will cover various aspects of staying safe and maintaining good health during your time in Greece, from healthcare and emergency services to safety precautions and local considerations.

Healthcare in Greece

Greece has a well-developed healthcare system that provides quality medical care to residents and visitors. Here's what you need to know about healthcare in Greece:

1. **Public Healthcare**: Greece offers a public healthcare system known as the National Healthcare System (ESY). Citizens and legal residents are entitled to public healthcare services. If you are a legal resident, you may be eligible to access public healthcare as well.
2. **Private Healthcare**: Many expatriates and tourists opt for private healthcare services, which often provide faster access to medical care and a wider range of amenities. Private healthcare facilities are available in major cities and tourist destinations.
3. **Health Insurance**: It is advisable to have comprehensive health insurance that covers medical expenses during your stay in Greece. Ensure that your insurance plan includes coverage for emergencies, hospitalization, and repatriation if necessary.
4. **Pharmacies**: Pharmacies (or "pharmakeia") are common in Greece and can provide over-the-counter medications for minor ailments. Pharmacies also play a role in the healthcare system, as some medications are dispensed only with a prescription.
5. **Emergency Services**: In case of a medical emergency, dial 112 or 166 to reach the ambulance service. Greece has a well-

established emergency response system, and medical assistance is readily available.
6. **Vaccinations**: Greece does not require any specific vaccinations for entry. However, it's a good practice to ensure that your routine vaccinations, such as tetanus and hepatitis, are up to date.

Safety Precautions

Greece is generally a safe country for residents and tourists, but like anywhere else, it's important to take some safety precautions:

1. **Crime**: Greece has a low crime rate, but petty theft, such as pickpocketing, can occur in crowded tourist areas. Be cautious with your belongings, especially in busy places like public transportation and tourist attractions.
2. **Natural Disasters**: Greece is prone to earthquakes, particularly in certain regions. Familiarize yourself with earthquake safety measures, and follow any guidance provided by local authorities in case of tremors.
3. **Swimming Safety**: When swimming in the Mediterranean, pay attention to warning flags and currents. Follow lifeguard instructions and avoid swimming alone in remote areas.
4. **Sun Protection**: Greece enjoys a sunny climate, so it's important to protect yourself from the sun. Wear sunscreen, a hat, and sunglasses to avoid sunburn and heatstroke.
5. **Traffic Safety**: Greece has a relatively high rate of road accidents. Exercise caution when driving, adhere to speed limits, and avoid drinking and driving. In urban areas, watch out for pedestrians and scooters.

Local Considerations

Understanding and respecting local customs and traditions can contribute to your safety and integration in Greece:

1. **Social Etiquette**: Greeks value politeness and respect in social interactions. Greet people with a friendly "Kalimera" (good morning), "Kalispera" (good evening), or "Kalinihta" (good night).
2. **Public Behavior**: Avoid loud or disruptive behavior in public places, as it may be considered impolite.
3. **Dress Modestly**: When visiting churches, monasteries, or traditional villages, dress modestly by covering shoulders and knees. This applies to both men and women.
4. **Greetings**: Handshakes are a common form of greeting in Greece. When entering a room or meeting someone, offer a handshake. Close friends and family may greet each other with a kiss on both cheeks.
5. **Photography**: Always ask for permission before taking photos of individuals, especially in rural areas or during religious ceremonies.
6. **Smoking**: Smoking is prohibited in indoor public places, including restaurants and bars. Outdoor smoking areas are designated in some places.

Emergency Contacts

Knowing the emergency contact numbers in Greece is essential for your safety and peace of mind:

- **Emergency Services**: Dial 112 for general emergencies, including police, fire, and medical assistance.
- **Police**: Dial 100 for police assistance.
- **Fire Brigade**: Dial 199 for fire-related emergencies.
- **Ambulance**: Dial 166 for medical emergencies and ambulance services.
- **Tourist Police**: In major tourist destinations, there are tourist police offices with officers who can assist tourists in various

languages.

Health and Well-being

Maintaining good health and well-being while living in Greece involves a balanced approach:

1. **Healthy Diet**: Embrace the Mediterranean diet, rich in fresh fruits, vegetables, whole grains, and olive oil. Enjoy the local cuisine, but also maintain a balanced diet.
2. **Physical Activity**: Take advantage of Greece's outdoor beauty and engage in regular physical activity, such as hiking, swimming, or cycling.
3. **Medical Check-ups**: Schedule regular medical check-ups with a local healthcare provider to monitor your health and well-being.
4. **Mental Health**: Prioritize your mental health and seek support if needed. Greece has mental health professionals and resources available.
5. **Hydration**: Stay well-hydrated, especially during the hot summer months.
6. **Prescription Medications**: If you have any prescription medications, ensure that you have an adequate supply and a copy of your prescription.

Environmental Considerations

Greece's climate and natural beauty are part of its allure, but they also require some environmental considerations:

1. **Waste Management**: Follow local waste disposal regulations, including recycling. Many areas have separate bins for different types of waste.
2. **Water Conservation**: Be mindful of water conservation, particularly during the summer when water scarcity can be an

issue.
3. **Wildlife Protection**: Respect wildlife and natural habitats. Avoid disturbing or feeding animals in protected areas.

Conclusion

Staying safe and healthy while living in Greece is largely a matter of common sense and respect for local customs and regulations. Greece offers a welcoming environment with access to quality healthcare and a relatively low crime rate.

By taking precautions, understanding local norms, and prioritizing your well-being, you can fully enjoy the Greek lifestyle, the natural beauty of the country, and the warmth of its people.

Kalí ygeía! (Good health!)

Navigating Daily Life

Living in Greece provides a unique opportunity to immerse yourself in the Mediterranean lifestyle, filled with vibrant traditions, beautiful landscapes, and a relaxed pace of life. In this chapter, we'll explore the various aspects of daily life in Greece, including transportation, housing, shopping, and more, to help you adapt and enjoy your new home to the fullest.

Transportation

Getting around Greece is relatively easy, thanks to its well-developed transportation infrastructure:

1. **Public Transportation**: Greece offers extensive public transportation options, including buses, trams, and metro systems in major cities like Athens and Thessaloniki. Public transport is generally efficient and affordable.
2. **Taxis**: Taxis are readily available in urban areas. Ensure the taxi has a working meter, or agree on a fare before starting your journey.
3. **Ferries**: If you live on an island, ferries are a common mode of transportation between islands and the mainland. Ferry schedules can vary by season, so plan your trips accordingly.
4. **Car Rentals**: If you plan to explore rural areas, renting a car is a convenient option. Greece has an extensive road network, and driving can be an enjoyable way to discover the countryside.
5. **Biking and Walking**: In many cities and towns, walking and biking are popular modes of transportation, especially for short distances.

Housing

Finding the right housing in Greece depends on your preferences, budget, and location. Here are some housing options to consider:

1. **Apartments**: Apartments are the most common housing type in urban areas. They vary in size and amenities, from small studios to spacious apartments.
2. **Houses**: If you prefer more space and privacy, you can find houses for rent in suburban or rural areas.
3. **Island Living**: On Greek islands, accommodations range from charming cottages and apartments to luxury villas and resorts, catering to various budgets and preferences.
4. **Short-Term Rentals**: Short-term rentals through platforms like Airbnb are prevalent in tourist destinations and provide flexibility for temporary stays.
5. **Real Estate Agents**: Utilize local real estate agents to help you find housing that meets your criteria. They can assist with negotiations and paperwork.
6. **Legal Requirements**: Be aware of legal requirements for renting or purchasing property in Greece, which may include permits and tax obligations.

Utilities and Services
Setting up utilities and services in Greece is straightforward:

1. **Electricity and Water**: Electricity and water services are reliable and accessible in most areas. Utility bills are typically paid monthly or bimonthly.
2. **Internet and TV**: High-speed internet and cable or satellite TV services are readily available, with various providers and packages to choose from.
3. **Mobile Phone**: Greece has extensive mobile phone coverage. You can easily obtain a SIM card from local providers to access mobile services.
4. **Postal Services**: The Hellenic Post (ELTA) offers postal and courier services, including mail delivery and package shipping.

Grocery Shopping and Markets

Grocery shopping in Greece is a delightful experience, with access to fresh and local products:

1. **Supermarkets**: Large supermarket chains like AB Vassilopoulos, Sklavenitis, and Lidl are common and offer a wide range of products, including fresh produce, dairy, and household items.
2. **Local Markets**: Many neighborhoods have local markets, known as "laiki agora," where you can purchase fresh fruits, vegetables, and seafood directly from local farmers and producers.
3. **Bakeries**: Greek bakeries, or "fournoi," are known for their fresh bread, pastries, and savory pies. Try "koulouri" (sesame-covered bread rings) and "tiropita" (cheese pie).
4. **Butcher Shops**: Local butcher shops, or "kreas," offer a variety of meats, including lamb, pork, and poultry.
5. **Specialty Stores**: Explore specialty stores for items like olives, olive oil, cheese, and herbs. Local delis, known as "charcuteries," offer cured meats and traditional sausages.

Dining and Eating Out

Eating out is a significant part of Greek culture, and you'll find a wide range of dining options:

1. **Tavernas**: Tavernas are traditional Greek restaurants that serve local dishes in a relaxed setting. They are known for their warm hospitality and often feature live music.
2. **Kafenia**: Kafenia are traditional coffeehouses where locals gather to enjoy coffee, play tavli (backgammon), and socialize. They may also serve light snacks and meze.
3. **Cafes and Bakeries**: Cafes and bakeries are ideal for enjoying a coffee and pastry or a light meal. Try "frappe" (iced coffee) or

"bougatsa" (sweet pastry).
4. **Restaurants**: Greece offers a diverse culinary scene with restaurants serving international cuisine, seafood, and gourmet dishes.
5. **Street Food**: Street food vendors offer delicious treats like "souvlaki" (skewered meat), "gyros" (rotisserie meat), and "koulouri" (sesame bread rings).

Language and Communication

Greek is the official language of Greece, but English is widely spoken, especially in tourist areas and larger cities. Learning some basic Greek phrases can enhance your daily interactions and help you navigate daily life.

Banking and Finance

Banking and financial services are accessible and straightforward in Greece:

1. **Bank Accounts**: You can open a bank account in Greece by providing the required documentation, such as proof of residence and identification.
2. **ATMs**: ATMs are widely available and accept international debit and credit cards. However, it's advisable to inform your bank of your travel plans to avoid card issues.
3. **Currency**: Greece uses the Euro (EUR) as its official currency.
4. **Online Banking**: Most Greek banks offer online banking services, making it easy to manage your finances remotely.

Education

If you have school-age children, Greece provides various education options:

1. **Public Schools**: Greece has a public education system that is free for Greek citizens and legal residents. Instruction is in

Greek, and the curriculum follows Greek standards.
2. **International Schools**: International schools offer education in various languages and follow international curricula. They are ideal for expatriate families and provide continuity in education.
3. **Language Support**: If your child is not fluent in Greek, some schools offer language support programs to help them integrate.

Recreation and Leisure

Greece offers a wide range of recreational activities to enjoy during your free time:

1. **Beaches**: Greece is renowned for its beautiful beaches, offering opportunities for swimming, sunbathing, and water sports.
2. **Outdoor Activities**: Explore the stunning landscapes of Greece by hiking, biking, or exploring national parks and natural reserves.
3. **Cultural Events**: Attend cultural events, including festivals, concerts, and theater performances, to immerse yourself in Greek arts and traditions.
4. **Sports**: Engage in sports and fitness activities, including soccer, basketball, tennis, and yoga.
5. **Nightlife**: Greece's nightlife scene comes alive after dark, with vibrant bars, clubs, and live music venues.

Legal and Administrative Matters

Living in Greece may involve various administrative tasks and legal requirements:

1. **Residence Permit**: If you plan to live in Greece long-term, you may need to obtain a residence permit. Requirements vary depending on your nationality and the purpose of your stay.

2. **Taxes**: Understand the Greek tax system and your tax obligations, including income tax, property tax, and value-added tax (VAT).
3. **Driving License**: If you plan to drive in Greece, ensure that your driving license is valid and meets Greek requirements.
4. **Voting**: If you are an EU citizen, you may have the right to vote in local elections in Greece.
5. **Legal Assistance**: For legal matters, consider seeking assistance from a local attorney or legal advisor familiar with Greek law.

Conclusion

Navigating daily life in Greece is a rewarding experience filled with cultural discoveries, culinary delights, and the beauty of the Mediterranean lifestyle. By familiarizing yourself with local customs, taking advantage of transportation options, and embracing the welcoming spirit of the Greek people, you can create a fulfilling and enjoyable life in this enchanting country.

Καλή ζωή! (Good life!)

Enjoying Your Greek Adventure

Congratulations! You've embarked on an exciting journey by moving to Greece. This Mediterranean paradise offers a wealth of experiences, from stunning landscapes and ancient history to delicious cuisine and warm hospitality. In this chapter, we'll explore how to make the most of your Greek adventure, ensuring that your time in this beautiful country is filled with memorable moments and meaningful connections.

Exploring the Greek Islands

Greece is famous for its picturesque islands, each with its own unique charm. Consider island-hopping to discover the diverse beauty of the Greek archipelago:

1. **Santorini**: Known for its iconic sunsets, white-washed buildings, and crystal-clear waters, Santorini is a must-visit destination. Explore the villages of Fira and Oia, relax on the beaches, and savor local wines.
2. **Mykonos**: Mykonos is renowned for its vibrant nightlife, beautiful beaches, and cosmopolitan atmosphere. Spend your days on the beach and your nights exploring the island's clubs and bars.
3. **Crete**: Greece's largest island offers a mix of ancient history, charming villages, and stunning landscapes. Explore the Palace of Knossos, hike the Samaria Gorge, and indulge in Cretan cuisine.
4. **Rhodes**: With its medieval Old Town, beautiful beaches, and historic sites, Rhodes is a blend of culture and relaxation. Don't miss the Palace of the Grand Master and the Acropolis of Rhodes.
5. **Corfu**: Corfu, with its lush greenery and Venetian architecture, is a haven for nature lovers and history enthusiasts. Visit the Old Town, hike through olive groves, and

enjoy the island's traditional cuisine.
6. **Zakynthos**: Known for the Shipwreck Beach (Navagio), Zakynthos is a stunning island with turquoise waters and dramatic landscapes. Take a boat tour to the famous shipwreck, visit Blue Caves, and enjoy the local hospitality.

Outdoor Adventures

Greece's diverse landscapes offer numerous opportunities for outdoor adventures:

1. **Hiking**: Explore Greece's beautiful trails and mountainous regions. Hike the Zagori trails in Epirus, trek to the top of Mount Olympus, or follow ancient paths in Crete's Samaria Gorge.
2. **Water Sports**: Enjoy a variety of water sports, including snorkeling, scuba diving, windsurfing, and paddleboarding. The Greek islands offer excellent conditions for these activities.
3. **Cycling**: Discover the countryside and coastal regions on two wheels. Many areas have cycling routes suitable for both beginners and experienced cyclists.
4. **Sailing**: Consider renting a sailboat or joining a sailing tour to explore secluded coves and hidden gems along the coast.
5. **Skiing**: In the winter, Greece's mountainous regions offer skiing and snowboarding opportunities. Parnassos and Kalavrita are popular ski destinations.

Cultural Immersion

Immerse yourself in Greek culture and traditions to truly embrace your adventure:

1. **Local Festivals**: Participate in local festivals and celebrations, such as the Carnival of Patras, Easter in Corfu, and the Athens Epidaurus Festival.

2. **Greek Music and Dance**: Attend live performances of traditional Greek music and dance. Learn to dance the syrtaki or zeibekiko at local dance classes.
3. **Greek Language**: Continue to learn and practice the Greek language to enhance your cultural understanding and connect with locals.
4. **Cooking Classes**: Join cooking classes to master the art of Greek cuisine. Learn to prepare traditional dishes like moussaka, tzatziki, and baklava.
5. **Historical Sites**: Explore Greece's rich history by visiting archaeological sites, ancient theaters, and museums. Some must-see sites include the Acropolis in Athens, Delphi, and Epidaurus.

Local Experiences

To fully enjoy your Greek adventure, consider these local experiences:

1. **Visit a Kafenio**: Spend time in a traditional coffeehouse (kafenio) to enjoy Greek coffee and engage in conversations with locals.
2. **Relax at a Beach Taverna**: Savor fresh seafood and meze at a beachfront taverna while taking in the sea views.
3. **Take a Boat Tour**: Explore hidden caves, swim in crystal-clear waters, and visit remote islands on a boat tour.
4. **Enjoy Greek Wine**: Visit local wineries and vineyards to taste the diversity of Greek wines, including famous varieties like Assyrtiko and Xinomavro.
5. **Attend a Greek Wedding**: If you have the opportunity, attending a Greek wedding is a memorable cultural experience filled with music, dancing, and delicious food.

Building Relationships

Building relationships and connecting with locals is a fundamental part of enjoying your Greek adventure:

1. **Philoxenia**: Embrace Greek hospitality (philoxenia) by accepting invitations, participating in social gatherings, and building friendships with locals.
2. **Socialize**: Frequent local cafes, tavernas, and community events to meet people and become part of the community.
3. **Volunteer**: Consider volunteering for local initiatives or charitable organizations to give back to the community.
4. **Language Exchange**: Engage in language exchange programs to improve your Greek language skills and connect with Greek speakers.

Safety and Practical Considerations

While Greece is generally a safe country, it's essential to stay informed and take precautions:

1. **Emergency Contacts**: Familiarize yourself with local emergency contact numbers, including police (100), fire brigade (199), and medical emergencies (166).
2. **Travel Insurance**: Ensure you have comprehensive travel or health insurance to cover unforeseen events, including medical emergencies.
3. **Local Laws and Regulations**: Respect local laws and regulations, including customs and immigration requirements.
4. **Healthcare**: Stay proactive about your health by scheduling regular check-ups and vaccinations, if necessary.

Conclusion

Your Greek adventure is an opportunity to embrace the beauty, culture, and spirit of this remarkable country. By exploring its diverse landscapes, engaging in local traditions, and forming meaningful connections, you'll create lasting memories and a deep appreciation for Greece's unique way of life.

As you continue your journey, remember the Greek proverb: "I Kalí tihi!" (Good luck!)

Conclusion

Congratulations! You've reached the end of this comprehensive guide on how to move to Greece and embark on your Greek adventure. As you reflect on the wealth of information and insights you've gathered throughout this book, you should be feeling well-prepared and excited about the journey ahead. Moving to Greece is not just a change of location; it's a transformational experience that will enrich your life in many ways.

Your decision to move to Greece is a bold step that promises a life filled with stunning landscapes, a rich cultural heritage, and the warmth of Greek hospitality. This concluding chapter serves as a final guidepost, offering some parting thoughts, tips for a smooth transition, and a reminder of the wonderful opportunities that await you in this Mediterranean paradise.

Embrace the Adventure

Moving to a new country is an adventure, and Greece is no exception. It's a land of contrasts, where ancient history meets modernity, and bustling cities are just a stone's throw from tranquil villages. Your Greek adventure will be characterized by exploration, growth, and a deep connection to the local culture.

As you settle into your new life, remember to embrace the journey and remain open to the unexpected. Each day in Greece can bring new discoveries, whether it's stumbling upon a hidden beach, connecting with a local artisan, or savoring a dish you've never tried before. The more you immerse yourself in the Greek way of life, the richer your experience will be.

Cultural Sensitivity and Respect

One of the keys to a successful transition to life in Greece is cultural sensitivity and respect. While Greek culture is known for its warmth and hospitality, it also has its own customs and traditions. Taking the time to learn about and respect these cultural norms will go a long way in building positive relationships with locals.

Greeks appreciate when newcomers make an effort to understand and participate in their traditions. Whether it's celebrating Easter with a midnight church service or learning a few basic Greek phrases to communicate with your neighbors, these gestures demonstrate your genuine interest in becoming a part of the community.

Maintaining Connections

While embarking on a new adventure often means leaving behind familiar faces and places, it's important to maintain connections with loved ones from your home country. In today's interconnected world, it's easier than ever to stay in touch through video calls, social media, and messaging apps.

Additionally, consider joining expatriate communities or local clubs and groups to meet fellow expats who share your interests and experiences. Building a support network in Greece can provide a sense of belonging and camaraderie, especially during the initial adjustment period.

Exploring Beyond Your Comfort Zone

Moving to a new country is an opportunity to step outside your comfort zone and challenge yourself in new ways. It's a chance to discover hidden talents, develop resilience, and adapt to different environments. Embrace this growth and transformation as you navigate the ups and downs of expat life.

Whether it's learning a new language, trying your hand at a new hobby, or navigating the intricacies of Greek bureaucracy, each challenge you overcome will contribute to your personal development. In the end, you'll emerge from the experience with a greater sense of self and an expanded worldview.

The Joys of Greek Cuisine

One of the most delightful aspects of living in Greece is undoubtedly the cuisine. Greek food is a celebration of fresh ingredients, bold flavors, and time-honored recipes. It's an invitation to savor every meal and enjoy the simple pleasure of good company.

As you explore the diverse world of Greek cuisine, don't hesitate to try new dishes and savor local specialties. Whether you're indulging in a traditional Greek meze with friends, enjoying a leisurely taverna dinner by the sea, or sipping on a Greek coffee at a local kafenio, every culinary experience is an opportunity to connect with the heart of Greek culture.

Appreciating the Mediterranean Lifestyle

The Mediterranean lifestyle is more than just a way of living; it's a philosophy that prioritizes balance, community, and the enjoyment of life's simple pleasures. Living in Greece provides a front-row seat to this way of life, where the pace is unhurried, relationships are cherished, and nature is a source of inspiration.

Take the time to savor leisurely meals with loved ones, enjoy the beauty of the Mediterranean landscapes, and embrace the importance of relaxation and well-being. Whether you're strolling along the cobblestone streets of a Greek village, basking in the warmth of the Mediterranean sun, or sipping on a glass of Greek wine under a starry sky, these are the moments that define the Mediterranean lifestyle.

Facing Challenges with Resilience

While the Greek adventure is filled with wonder and beauty, it's important to acknowledge that it may also come with its fair share of challenges. Whether it's navigating Greek bureaucracy, adjusting to a different healthcare system, or encountering language barriers, each challenge is an opportunity to grow and adapt.

Approach challenges with patience, resilience, and a problem-solving mindset. Seek support from local resources, expat communities, and friends. Remember that many expats have faced similar challenges and have successfully overcome them, and you can too.

Leaving a Legacy

As you build a life in Greece, consider the legacy you'll leave behind. Your time in this beautiful country can be marked not only by personal fulfillment but also by contributions to the community and the environment.

Participate in local initiatives, support causes you're passionate about, and engage in sustainable practices that protect the natural beauty of Greece for future generations. Your actions, no matter how small, can make a positive impact and leave a lasting legacy in your adopted homeland.

A Lifetime of Memories

Your journey to Greece is more than a temporary relocation; it's an opportunity to create a lifetime of memories. Whether you're exploring ancient ruins, sharing laughter with new friends, or simply enjoying the Mediterranean breeze on your balcony, cherish every moment of your Greek adventure.

The experiences you gather, the connections you make, and the lessons you learn will become part of your personal story. As you look back on your time in Greece, you'll fondly recall the people you met, the places you explored, and the profound sense of fulfillment that comes from living life to the fullest.

A New Beginning

Moving to Greece is not just about changing your address; it's about embarking on a new beginning. It's a chance to reinvent yourself, to embrace a different way of life, and to savor the beauty of the world around you. It's a reminder that life is a journey, and each new chapter is an opportunity to write a compelling and meaningful story.

As you step into this new beginning, carry with you the wisdom and experiences you've gained from this guide. Be open to the unexpected, stay true to your sense of adventure, and embrace the gift of living in Greece with an open heart and an eager spirit.

Your Greek adventure awaits. Seize it with enthusiasm, curiosity, and gratitude, and may your days in Greece be filled with love, laughter, and the magic of this extraordinary country.

Καλό ταξίδι και καλή τύχη! (Bon voyage and good luck!)

Appendix: Resources and Useful Information

In your journey to relocate to Greece and embrace the Mediterranean dream, it's essential to have access to valuable resources and information. This appendix provides a curated list of resources, websites, and contacts to help you navigate various aspects of your move and life in Greece. From government agencies to expat communities, these sources can be valuable references throughout your adventure.

Government and Legal Information:

1. **Greek Ministry of Foreign Affairs**: www.mfa.gr[1] - Official information on visas, residence permits, and consular services for foreign nationals.
2. **Greek Consulates and Embassies**: Locate your nearest Greek consulate or embassy for assistance with visa applications and legal matters.
3. **Greek National Tourism Organization**: www.visitgreece.gr[2] - A wealth of information on travel, culture, and tourism in Greece.
4. **Hellenic Police**: www.astynomia.gr[3] - Information on police services and emergency contacts in Greece.

Real Estate and Housing:

1. **Hellenic Association of Realtors**: www.sekd.gr[4] - Connect with licensed real estate agents and access property listings in Greece.

---

1. https://chat.openai.com/c/www.mfa.gr
2. https://chat.openai.com/c/www.visitgreece.gr
3. https://chat.openai.com/c/www.astynomia.gr
4. https://chat.openai.com/c/www.sekd.gr

2. **Airbnb**: www.airbnb.com[5] - Explore temporary accommodation options while you search for a permanent home in Greece.

Healthcare and Medical Services:

1. **National Organization for Healthcare Services Provision (EOPYY)**: www.eopyy.gov.gr[6] - Information on public healthcare services in Greece.
2. **Greek National Tourism Organization - Medical Tourism**: www.visitgreece.gr/medicaltourism[7] - Details on medical facilities and services for expatriates and medical tourists.

Education and Schools:

1. **Ministry of Education and Religious Affairs**: www.minedu.gov.gr[8] - Information on the Greek education system and international schools.

Employment and Entrepreneurship:

1. **Greek Manpower Employment Organization (OAED)**: www.oaed.gr[9] - Employment services, job listings, and information for job seekers and employers.
2. **Hellenic Entrepreneurship Award**: www.hellenic-award.com[10] - Support and funding opportunities for entrepreneurs and startups in Greece.

---

5. https://chat.openai.com/c/www.airbnb.com

6. https://chat.openai.com/c/www.eopyy.gov.gr

7. https://chat.openai.com/c/www.visitgreece.gr/medicaltourism

8. https://chat.openai.com/c/www.minedu.gov.gr

9. https://chat.openai.com/c/www.oaed.gr

10. https://chat.openai.com/c/www.hellenic-award.com

A GUIDE TO RELOCATING TO GREECE

Expatriate Communities and Support:

1. **Expats in Greece**: www.expatsingreece.com[11] - Online community and forum for expatriates in Greece, offering advice, support, and networking opportunities.
2. **InterNations Greece**: www.internations.org/greece-expats[12] - A global expat community with local chapters in Greece, facilitating social and professional connections.

Language Learning:

1. **Duolingo**: www.duolingo.com[13] - An online language learning platform with Greek language courses.
2. **Hellenic American Union**: www.hau.gr[14] - Offers Greek language courses and cultural programs for expatriates.

Transportation:

1. **Hellenic Civil Aviation Authority**: www.ypa.gr[15] - Information on airports, flights, and travel regulations in Greece.
2. **Hellenic Railways Organization (OSE)**: www.ose.gr[16] - Details on train services and schedules in Greece.

Cultural and Tourist Information:

1. **Greek National Opera**: www.nationalopera.gr[17] - Information

---

11. https://chat.openai.com/c/www.expatsingreece.com
12. https://chat.openai.com/c/www.internations.org/greece-expats
13. https://chat.openai.com/c/www.duolingo.com
14. https://chat.openai.com/c/www.hau.gr
15. https://chat.openai.com/c/www.ypa.gr
16. https://chat.openai.com/c/www.ose.gr

on cultural events, performances, and tickets.
2. **Greek National Tourism Organization**: www.visitgreece.gr[18] - Explore Greece's cultural heritage, tourist destinations, and events.

Conclusion:

This list is intended to serve as a starting point for your journey as you relocate to Greece. Be sure to explore additional resources specific to your needs and interests, and don't hesitate to reach out to local expat communities and organizations for support and guidance. Embracing the Mediterranean dream is an adventure that can be enriched by tapping into the wealth of information and assistance available to you.

As you embark on this exciting chapter of your life, remember that Greece is a land of beauty, culture, and warm hospitality. Embrace the opportunities it offers, build lasting connections, and savor every moment of your Mediterranean adventure.

Καλό ταξίδι! (Bon voyage!)

---

17. https://chat.openai.com/c/www.nationalopera.gr

18. https://chat.openai.com/c/www.visitgreece.gr

www.ingramcontent.com/pod-product-compliance
Lightning Source LLC
LaVergne TN
LVHW042156070526
838201LV00047BA/1431